Basics
Of
Business

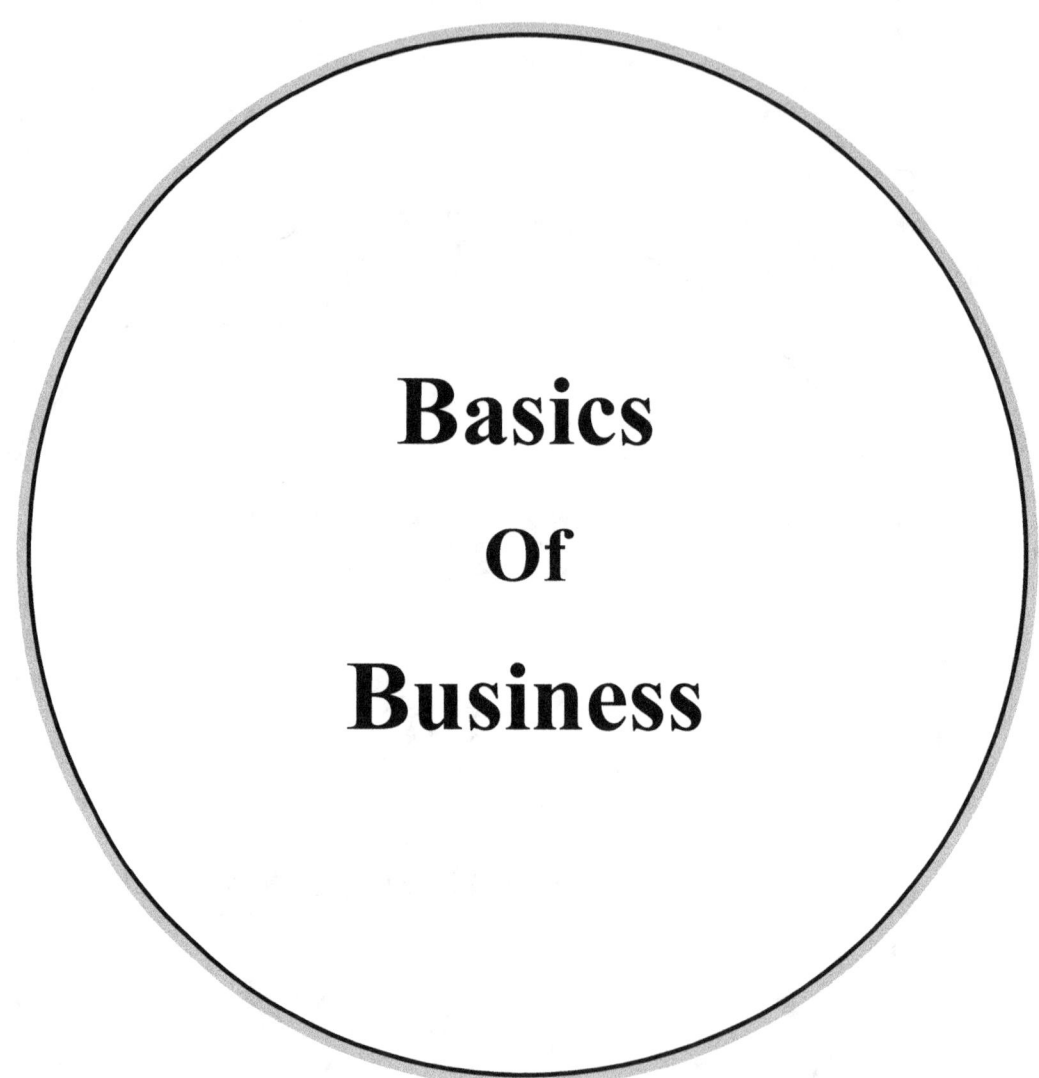

Basics
Of
Business

ANTHONY MORGAN

Published by Lulu Publishing

Copywright©Anthony Morgan 2017

All rights reserved. No part of this publication may be reproduced, stored in a retrieval system or transmitted, in any form or by any means, electric, mechanical, photocopy, recording or otherwise without the prior permission of the author.

First published in the United States of America by Lulu Publishing

Cover design and image by Rodesign

Table of Contents

i. Introduction ....
ii. What's cooking? ....
iii. E-Commerce ....
iv. Business Plan ....
v. Business Ethics ....
vi. Taxes/corporate structure ....
vii. Selecting Business Insurance ....
viii. Marketing ....
ix. Financial processing ....
x. Funding ....
xi. Final entrepreneurial questions ....
xii. Glossary ....
xiii. Bibliography ....

Preface

When I first started this project basics of business, it simple design and how it was written was for my provost to get in to the doctoral program for business in college.

I wrote a little more and compiled a ton of information from a variety of sources. Some sources from fortune 500 companies and others who were the mom and pop generation in the business world of today.

I was sitting at my computer sifting through all of the documentation of people who had failed at business, and we're reaching out to online forums trying to gather information that could garner them some type of success as a business's owner. I also sifted through information about new business owners that the best success they could hope for.

The one thing that hit me was the category that I fell into and that's business failure. So, a lot of the information that I have compiled came from over a decade of refusing to "just give up," but also if there was just a basic guide, something easy to understand, then maybe people could reach their potential as business owners.

So, I dumbed it down thinking that if I could've just had someone give me the basics on what I needed, then just maybe there would have been a possibility of success. However, I don't consider myself a failure by any means, at the time I attempted to open a business I had what was considered a worker's knowledge.

While having an extensive experience in the field you're trying to break in to can help it can also hurt you. You've got to be able to set yourself aside from the actual worker mentality, while understanding that without employee respect you could fall fast in business.

So, I put together this guide to help the new business owner understand that opening a business of any model is a commitment, to your success, your business's success, your home life, and your ethics. It's the not knowing where to start or take that grand idea that you have that motivated me to open up what could be considered bad information or I just don't know enough.

Well let me explain it to you this way, I hold a degree in business, I've failed at business, I've succeed in business and yet I'll never give up sharing the information I learn or have learned over the years because of critics.

This guide is for the dreamer, the one day I mightiers, and the ones who everyone else says "you just can't get it done," I'm here to tell you, "yes you can!"

We must remember that we learn from our mistakes and one, who says they've never made a mistake in business, has never been in business. Mistakes make us stronger when we can identify them and correct them, no one is a failure in business because you've already taken a step many are afraid to take; with that I welcome all of the new business owners of tomorrow to the business world of today and wish you much luck, this is for you and you taking that first step.

Anthony Morgan

Acknowledgements

This guide to business is dedicated to my father who encouraged me to try and try some more whether it be getting published, being a successful business owner, or educating as a profession.

Dennis Arnold Morgan Sr.

My father, grandfather, and a best friend too many, a truly special breed of person!

1945-2013

Left Blank Intentionally..............

Introduction

The basics of business!

My name is Anthony Morgan I'm going to cover your basics of how to start a business. First of all, let's get a few things out in the open. Anyone can start a business on very little; well structure your business that is.

Some of your basics are going to be what type of structure you are going to make your business... (I.e.... LLC, S-Corporation, C-corporation, etc.) In North Carolina where I'm from this is a modest fee of $125.00.

What does this get you once you've begun, what's known as the sectary of state paperwork filing plus its fees? You my friend have just moved beyond the idea mode, the I wish someone would click on my social media page, and now your friends can stop talking about you behind your back about, "I don't know why I've got so and so's crazy idea on my page."

So, this is a process of utilizing very little of your own pocket cash and gaining capital in other areas. However, there is no free in the start of any business, just a multitude of short cuts that can be taken and that are all legal.

Of course, you should have an idea of what type of business you want to open and if it's going to take a 100,000 to get there start cuddling up to your rich Uncle or parent to make them, what I like to call investors but try and always have one real business partner. You want one person that no matter what happens in the business or the business falls is going to want to talk about restructuring and trying to make a move again.

Some of your most important items to a successful business are going to be text book and common sense must haves.

Examples are, you are going to want consumers or business owners to be able to find you, so they will do what everyone else in this digital age does, and they're going to the internet. I would say you had better have an online presence because if you can't type your business name in a search engine and get a result; your legitimately will come in to question.

I already know what you're thinking, "this is going to cost me a small fortune," well yes and no. Having a business doesn't mean you create a catchy name and make a buck and then sit back with your feet propped up on the desk giving people orders now. It does however mean that you can say you're an entrepreneur.

I know that the amount of information that I'm giving you can be somewhat overwhelming but there is good news.

I'm going to break it all down for you, bit by bit and you don't even need a high-priced degree in business for that. I went ahead and got the high-priced degree and the student debt for both of us.

A few things that you'll need to understand as we get started. Never let anyone including yourself tells you that this can't be done. The instructions are easy to follow and there will be incorporation reference material for you in the back. I will also give you a break down on marketing vs digital marketing, why I recommend WordPress, Google AdWords and how it's effective, business credit the reason why it's a must, Dunn and Bradstreet, the IRS and why you should never get stuck in the 1099 trap.

All very easy stuff and no step skipped. I will also have another project coming out hopefully by November how to jumpstart your non-profit. I know who would want to not make a profit but a non-profit is a business nonetheless that pays employees too.

Chapter One

What's Cooking?

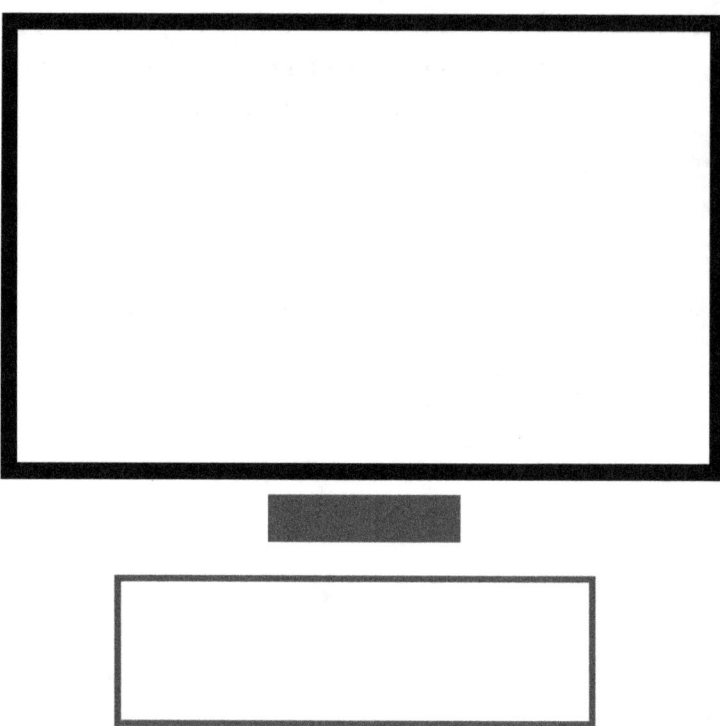

Where do I start? This is usually the most common question that is asked when new entupenure attempt to take on their first business or become self employed.

The oddest part about this question is it can be answered in a few different ways. For example, where do you want to see you and your business in the short term and the long term? What goals are you trying to achieve from being a business owner? Then there's my answer, the secatary of state.

Basics of Business

My answer will always be the secatary of state but wait I'm going to give you the reason, the methodology, the madness behind it; it's called the mind's eye. Everyone has a mind's eye and that eye has created a map, the map leads you to the cleasha lightbulb and when that lightbulb gets turned on you start to create a brain stew.

I guess basically what I'm trying to say is your idea should already have been cooking, you should already be at your brain stew point. You the creator of your business should have thought of the following.

- Name
- market value
- Consumer (what type of consumer are you targeting, the public or business to business)
- Marketing
- The dreded financial plausibility

This is just a few of the ingredients needed to begin your brain stew. Once you've begun to jot down a couple of notes using these five ingredients, you'll soon find yourself adding things to your list and Wala before you know it you've got full blown brain stew.

This process usually takes anywhere between 60-90 days, of course it also depends on how motivated you the future business owner are. The way I figure it if you want something bad enough then you will find yourself donating more and more and more time to your goal at hand.

You should have by now also considered product and how you intend to produce, purchase, and sell your product(s). Most new small business owners take aim at being what is known as service proffenolls or providers. This is common for a specific tax structure known as either self employed or sole proprietor; Service providers that are commonly associated with this structure are:

- Lawn care professionals
- Window Washers

- Child care
- Gutter cleaners
- Pressure washer

This is just a few low cost and no tax structure businesses that are common today. However, if you choose either to become self employed, sole proprietor, or a corporation you still have the burden of state, local, and federal taxes that must be paid. The only difference is when you pay, whether it's quarterly, semiannual, or anual.

Okay now that we've began to stew, I hope you can understand why the first step should be the secatary of state corporations division. In order to file this paperwork properly, I would recommend outsourcing it to an online company; these are autofill forms so they are mistake proof (usually). Outsourcing to an online vendor for state paperwork does a few things, it list the online vendor as your general agent which you can change at a later date if needed, most often you can get a free trial and utize the free trial to have your paperwork done at cost. However, for some online vendors I can tell you this, it does pay to retain their $40-70 a month Service if it is something that your going to need every month but if it's something that you're going to use acially then utilize the trial membership for what it is, a trial.

Once you've started your state corporate paperwork and you have a clear idea of what type of business you are looking to start; this comes from our brain stew, we can then look forward at a document that you'll need to get from the IRS.

You will need to obtain an E.I.N or a tax ID number, this will identify the structure of your business and how you will pay your taxes; (I.e. quarterly, annually, semiannually, etc.) This document is also important because it will be the deciding factor in whether or not you will be issued a line of business credit.

Business basics takes you to the simpfied documents that are needed before you can intitate a business license in your local municipality. Although, you are new to the business world, the laws can not and should not be taken lightly nor should try to short cut them. Adhering to the letter of the law does a few things:

> ➤ Generates creditability
> ➤ You avoid costly mistakes
> ➤ You also have the ability to avoid business pitfalls.

Understanding that certain laws whether they be tax laws or local regulations early on gives you an advantage from many standpoints. For example, if you're light on capital and have not taken the time to write down your ingredients to your brain stew. You should probably at this point stop and begin writing down what your mind's eye is trying to tell you, follow the map, everything is obtainable and doable if you are willing to put the work in.

If we revisit the employer identification number (E.I.N or tax ID number) and its importance, you will soon understand that you don't want to be in debt to the government for taxes and you want to generate capital wherever you can.

There is a difference in generating any captial just to have capital and generating captial that can be used soley for the purpose of your business.

For example, if you are a chemical manufacturing start up you're going to begin looking for personal protective equipment for your employees; this equipment can get costly. So, the obvious soultation would be to find a vendor that offers this equipment with easy credit terms, such as net 10, 15, 20, or 30 these terms are the amount of days you must pay your invoice for the products that you ordered and received.

These types of terms are not available to new business owners that have not obtained their tax ID number or employer identification number (E.I.N). This number is essentially a key component to your businesses success, I mean after all you're not doing it for bragging rights alone, your doing this to be successful in your new business.

Let's do a small recap before we continue, you should have a clear idea of what type of business you are aiming for, you should have some idea of market share, you should consider your business name, your business structure, and last but not least tax ID or employer identification number.

We covered some important points but now it's time to get the inin depth reason on your brain stew and understanding their impotantance as well as breaking down the benefits of incorpating or staying at the self employed or sole proprietor level.

The first time I was asked what was my market share was when I opened my first business, Abidance Staffing, keep in mind that I was just as you most likely are at this moment, I had no idea what i was doing, my premiums behind Abidance Staffing is I wanted to do something in my community that no one else was doing and that was help people who really just wanted to work.

I spoke earlier about business pitfalls well if you excute any idea blindly you will find unwanted pitfalls at every turn. I set out with just a great name, a great idea, and a sole proprietorship corporate status. I found that without an effective marketing plan, you will find yourself making a lot of cold calls with no revenue, no revenue means that your family, your home life is going to take a hit but even bigger than that your creditability takes a hit.

So, when asked what was my market share I stood there dumbfounded, not understanding what my response was supposed to be. I left with my creditability in question and questions about my ability to run my business; imagine my surprise that not giving an answer or the right answer could do so much damage to my start up. I quickly scrabbled trying to research market share," what is this market share and why do I need to know it so bad?"

Market share is exactly as it reads, pretty simple looking back on it now. Market share is the hyathetical question," can the market you are attempting to break in to afford another or is there enough business in your field, location, to share the wealth." Naturally since I was the only Staffing company in my town for nearly thirty miles, I thought this was a no brainier. I thought, perfect no competition, plenty of people who are in need of work, I got this, execpt the businesses in my town were already struggling, unemployment was at an all-time high and nobody was hiring anyone. In a nutshell, I the perfect market but no share because as a Staffing business we depended on other businesses to keep our business a float. Although, I had the workforce, I provided the drug screen, and background check businesses could not afford to retain my service, which at this point was failing fast.

I found myself adapting a new moto, it's one I still use to this day, when you decide to take that first step into the business world, you must be willing to move, adapt, and adjust to the current situation good or bad. I turned to the world-wide web trying to gain more recognition from people in the neghboring towns to call on me and my workforce. I'm thinking at this point who can say no to a company that is offering competitive wages, drug screen, background checks, what I got was a larger workforce because I was appealing to the worker not the business owners. I also checked my website making sure I was getting the traffic needed to make it worth while, what I found out later on really made me question my own ability.

This is the point when capital has begun to come out of pocket and that day comes when you use someone else computer to show them your website and pitch them about how great your business is but you can't find your website when you type in the keywords the only pages you find are when you type your company's name in or when you hit next and you find your website on page ten or twenty if you're lucky.

So, here I sat with a business that was failing fast, no customers, no revenue which in turn meant I was slowly running out of capital to stay a float. This stemmed from not either knowing what market share was or being able to understand market share research.

Understanding market share research and the market you are attempting to break in to are very important. It's important to understand that market share and market research has to go beyond looking in the phone book and counting how many businesses of a simliar niche are out there. Some of the resources you can use can be found at the department of labor or your state revenue department. Corporations must submit reports and these reports can give you a general idea of what the market is currently like.

One of the most important topics of your brain stew is going to be your consumer. If you've worked in the hospitality industry at all which I'm sure we all have at one point in our life; you probably already have the moto the customer is always right. No... No... No I just want to get that out right away. If you are targeting the public and a customer buys 8 hamburgers but he eats one after he leaves the restaurant, you're going to give him a free hamburger? The answer is yes a hamburger cost roughly .22 to make, so yes you lose fifty cents, come on, we have to account for labor, the electric or gas, the codaments, and packaging.

However, if a customer files a compliant against your best worker are you going to terminate their employment? No of course not, you will tell the customer you will take care of it, pull your worker to the side in view of the customer in they are still present and give them the impression that they have won, while you are doing nothing more than getting your workers side of the story.

With that being said, customers that will frequent your establishment frequently, you will want to deal with, get to know them as if they're your best friends, you want to know your customer by their first name. This in itself will increase your revenue if you treat your customers like a person and not a happy meal or an account number.

While you maybe thinking, I already know how I'm going to get this done; I'm going to service the public and service business owners. This type of methodology doesn't work unless you plan to deliver coffee, fast-food, etc. A line has to be drawn and you must be clear on who you intend on providing your products and/or services to.

Determine your customer base is important and one of the easiest part of the development of your business. For example, if you are investing 10,000.00 into a restaurant franchise and they are only selling pizza and subs; your customer base can range anywhere from the coming of age teenager to the family, the breakdown of your consumer will come from the specific location and your market share research.

If your market share research tells you that there is room for growth and higher revenue moving your early stage business to an underdeveloped new shopping center but it can't give you a consumer age range. Do you risk it by moving to the underdeveloped new shopping center or do you open your business in a shipping center that can give the information that you feel would better benefit your new business?

Take just a moment and remember that nothing in business is a for sure thing, except for the fact you're looking for finicial freedom through your own business. The best way to analyze the situation is the shopping center that can not provide an age group but look at what it does provide for you. It will provide a cenus track of how many families are in a two-mile area of the shopping center, this will give you some idea if you will have thirty something's or higher or ages fifteen to thirty visting your pizza and subs restaurant.

Understanding who your consumer and what your consumers age will be is crucial to business owners and their survival. The next example takes on the premiums of if we were to open a mobile shredding business. This is strictly a business to business sales operation. First, you should canvas your local area, examining your competition, prices, dependability, and longevity. When it comes to business to business sales you must become more competitive and you have to bring a certain "wow" factor to the table, after all you must convince a business to sign a contract and give them credit terms. The complexity of business to business sales requires a unique set of skills, someone that has contacts in places you may not have may be the success or failure of your business.

We're investing the same money that we invested in the pizza and subs restaurant franchise for the mobile shredding business. Since this business is mobile, you could park your mobile shredder at your home working out of a small home office but since it's business to business who would our target consumer be? The business that we would target would be privately held businesses such as, attorney's office, doctor's office, some banking institutions, etc. However, we may have cut our cost by having a home office and parking at our home; business to business sales requires a very aggressive marketing campaign. The capital that you saved from the home Office and parking at your home will need to be directed towards that ad campaign.

Basics of Business

The basic fundamentals of business are understanding how to balance multiple things at single time in any given moment. The skills that a new business owner can gain from mistakes or failure can be used as the building blocks to great success, as long as you can recongitize your mistakes and accept your failures. Success will not messaure you but learning from your mistakes and refusing to let failure define you is your greatest success.

Marketing... Marketing... Marketing this is so confusing digital, traditional which one is better for my business? Marketing is one of the biggest compents to any business's success, you don't buy that brand of soap just, because do you? Marketing is a strategy, almost like a well played opera or video game. Your business and its success depends a lot on many different variations of marketing, this could be as simple as keywords to a well orchestrated size, color, and shape of your business logo or name. When marketing comes into "our building blocks" sanacrio everything matters, from calming colors to eye popping logos to specialized fonts used to craft your unique business name.

Opening a business is like having a very well disciplined army, everything you do with your business represents you and should have a certain semitary to it. Take for example, if you have a logo that is just a circle in a calming color, we'll use blue with your business name in the middle what do you get from it?

Maybe a soothing feeling or trusting feeling because of the blue, the circle can represent global distribution, put your business name in the middle and you've instantly become a world leader, disturbor in your field. What if we could make our logo more complex, not by much just add a drop shadow and an inner glow and you've now become an emerging powerhouse in your business field that's doing well.

How did we get that information from such a basic logo and your business name? Your business name is you and you are now a brand but we've got to go beyond the scope of branding alone. The pshycology of human nature tells us what our psycie responds to whether it's colors, a rainy day, or a day full of sunshine, the common component is color. Rainy days are grey and dull no color just bla and while a day of sunshine or a cloudy day are blue, white, and yellow. Humans respond more to bright colors and associate them as calming, like a day at the beach or laying on the green grass with that someone special in your life.

I'm no psychologist but when it comes to marketing I like to think I'm pretty good. Marketing has been implementing the basics of psychology to draw consumers in to their products before the color television. This is also why a lover of art can look at Vincent vangogh's painting staring night and feel relaxed; it's not about understanding the art as much as it is staring at the blue and yellow of the painting.

When marketing your business, this is where you will really want to be creative, sleek, professional, yet you're going to want to appeal to your target audience but have your own voice in every part of your logo, font, and color and represent your consumer at the same time. One bad unreadable word can lead to disaster, a wrong color could lead to anger, or the worst of all is the words unprofessional or amerturish could follow.

If you're anything like me going to want to know why I didn't go in order. Well I went in order of priority, the list at the top gives you your first five ingredients to begin your brain stew; I then broke each down in order of what should take priority. What about the name, right?

Your business name is your identity in the business world, so what should you do with it? Brand...Brand...Brand and brand it some more, now you don't have to be primer world coffee or PWC you can be brand and butter advertising; your name is your name not a catch phrase it's what separates you from the rest. You really want to make sure you are one percent decided on your business name before moving forward with any documentation, if you decide to change it later this could be costly.

When I say costly, I'm talking about redoing state paperwork, IRS paperwork, letterhead, business cards, marketing and the list goes on. The changing of a business name is the same as starting a new business; no one knows the new name, your deadcated consumers may stop coming to your business for fear that you were forced out.

Chapter Two

E-commerce

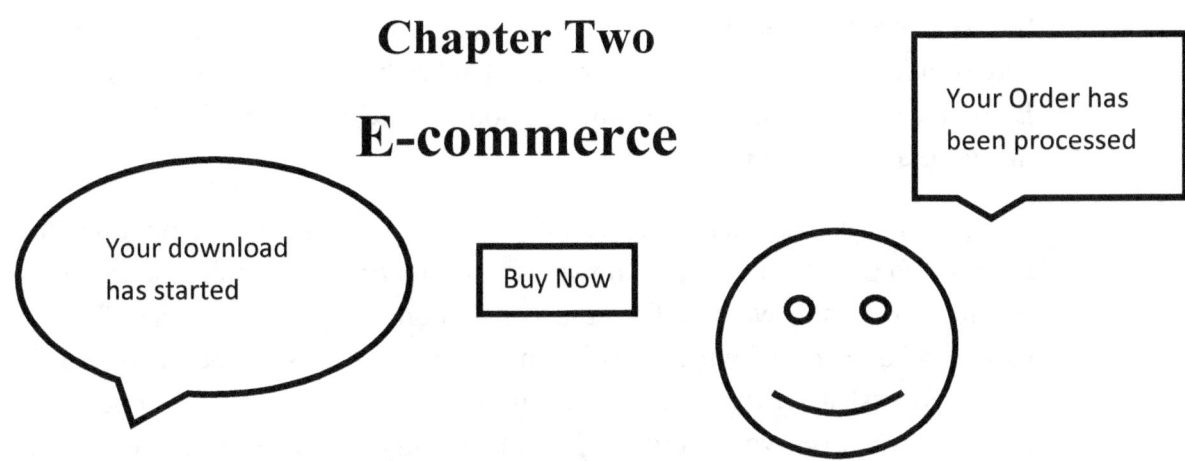

E-commerce, what a wonderful word, it is the power to become a business owner for as little as twenty-five bucks. The digital world we live in as transcended how we view businesses today as a whole as well as any one has the potential to become a business owner with just a little knowledge.

So, we talked about the importance of our brain stew and tax ID numbers as well as what our corporate status would be early on but fact is those who have a desire to become a business owner quickly will hunt for any and every type of short cut. I myself personally am a fan of what I call leap cuts, it's kinda like leap frog only we do it in the business world. E-commerce can be utilized best for a clear and decisive product (s) that you would like to sell to the public. However, I don't recommend e-commerce for business to business sales, only because if done incorrectly you will find yourself quickly over extending your personal funds.

Unfortunately, it will be difficult for you to utilize your personal banks merchant account Services at most financial institutions if you don't incorporate and have your state paperwork either processing or processed. Needless to say, there are gateways out there that can help you process payments without your corporate paperwork, these gateways are specifically designed for the self-employed or sole proprietor in mind, let's face it they make money when you make money.

So, what is e-commerce exactly? You already know the answer from the front end even if you've never opened a traditional brick and mortar business before. E-commerce is the purchase of sale or goods online, why would you consider this to be a business option?

The basics of business shows us that if you were to try and make extra revenue by selling a product at what is known as a flea market to a small amount of the public, then what if we used the same concept on a larger scale. What if you produced hand crafted wine racks in a multitude of colors, shapes, and sizes but your market share research tells you that the local market will not support such a business. However, you know that in wine country 200 miles away your business would hit the ground running and you would meet your forecast goals. You have to evaluate the situation are you going to go well I gave it a shot and walk away, trying to sell your well-crafted wine racks to friends and family until everyone has one or do you move, adapt, and adjust to the market and find a platform that you can garner exposure for your hard work without breaking the bank?

The simple answer is everyone that wants to be in business usually has the same goal and that is financial freedom. In order to achieve this goal, you've got to use the mindset that you're a multifaceted business. This means that you are going to have to be on an adaptable level. The next question that usually comes is what do I know about writing code, whether it's HTML, Java script, or CSS? Well in today's digital age there are simple e-commerce sites that provide you with what's known as the drag and drop method. This method can go a long way for the website creator novice that is unless you a spare 500.00 lying around that you can take away from your start up and hire someone to do it.

Although, e-commerce is an easy way to generate revenue for your business, like every business whether it's going to be in conjunction with a brick and mortar location, you've got to consider your web presence as if it is its own separate location. The platform you choose will make all the difference in the amount of traffic that is generated towards your online website.

Some of the key points to consider are how the search engines are going to read your web address, this is directly associated with something called permalinks. Also, choosing the proper keywords can transcend your profit to a loss, just as important is the search engine optimization, these components deal directly with the choice of platform and your knowledge with code.

When you begin the process of utilizing the internet to gain a profit, you have a few keys that will lead you to that goal. Obviously the most important is exposure or marketing and how you either want vendors or the public to see your website. The variables that you also must take into account are how the search engines are going to view your site. The search engine Google for example is a very blog friendly search engine, how can we utilize that information to our advantage.

Well simply put it's going to depend on the search engines favorite platform, and how you list your product (s) or services, take the platform WordPress as a premier example, this platform is easy to read, create, and the general design of WordPress eliminates the need for code because it uses extensions to formulate a website as if it were a blog.

The next step to this process is making sure you have effective hosting, hosting that's going to do the specific job it's designed to do, you've got to remember just because a hosting company says they can protect your business from online hackers, this may be true but should you put your trust in your hosting company or the gateway provider that's going to obtain your customer's information and your own?

Once you've chosen your platform, gateway, and whatever bells and whistles you want to add to your new web presence, it will take approximately three months to appear on the search engines, unless you've got a pretty aggressive advertising campaign backed up with SEO.

Although, a web presence is not required to open your new business but let's really be honest here, we want the consumer to have a quick and easy yet pleasant experience with your new business. With that being said, you don't have to have millions to play on the same playing field as fortune 500 companies. What is essentially the most important thing you can do is have functionality, when I say functionality I mean you want your consumer whether it is that you have a brick and mortar business or online only, you want clean crisp functional choices for your consumer. For example, you may have a business down town and you make the freshest bagels in town, you've solidified a consumer base; but they wish they had away to order your fresh bagels in advance. This creates the functionality of consumer convince and it also boost consumer confidence because now your customers are telling their friends how they order their bagels the day before, pick them up on the way to work and they're still hot and fresh.

This type of consumer confidence can triple your revenue, just from trying to offer a more convenient way to sell your product. Taking the first step to becoming a business owner is an examination of yourself, your ideas, and how to achieve your success whether it be online or a traditional business in a brick and mortar store.

The final topic about e-commerce is about your must haves, these must haves are something or than revenue generators. There are certain laws and terminology that apply only to e-commerce. When you first think of the idea of I'll sell online, it's easy, functional, low overhead, and I don't need employees to get started. This may true to some points of the e-commerce business owner but we've got to take other things into consideration.

Some of the key points that you will need to have in place are going to be, taxation, copyright laws, and consumer privacy. Whatever you sell online, consumer privacy needs to be too priority. You should ask yourself questions such as, "would I really buy from my business?" Especially if you are new to the business world, what if you're selling digital downloads or media, as a vendor you still must pay for the copyright or any reproduction of that or those products, otherwise you've just violated Federal law.

The last key point is what is known as the Nexus, the Nexus applies if you have a physical store front and an online e-commerce, if this is the case then in most states you must collect a state tax for every sale on every product. The notion behind this is no matter where the consumer buys the product (s) it is considered a purchase from your physical store front.

We've looked from a new business owner's perspective to try and get an understanding of how we can generate those much-loved profits but in order to really understand every aspect of your new e-commerce endeavor, you should always look at things from any and every angle. Although, many consumers lose the five senses when shopping online, we look at the gain of your consumer base because of simple conveniences offered by online vendors.

However, if we look at the real time financial stability of e-commerce you'll find that it's a low margin of actual business to consumer (B2C) the majority of credit transaction conducted on a digital platform are from business owners to other business owners or (B2B) trying to keep a steady supply of merchandise for their consumers. How has e-commerce changed how business owners purchase from other business owners?

Using a digital platform to maintain their supply and demand also saves existing business and new business owners a lot of capital. Using an online e-commerce source to bring in your inventory also gives you the business owner the functionality to keep your on-hand inventory at a low. This also gives the business owner a way to not only provide jobs to few employees if needed but it also helps the manufacture, the shipping company, and an array of other companies that help build the foundation for a shared profit growth.

Chapter three

The Business Plan

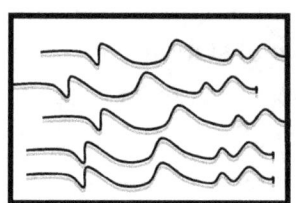 

Making sense of this thing called a business plan. So, what exactly is a business plan? A business plan a breakdown, step by step guide, or map to show the basic pros and cons of your business and why your business stands apart from all the rest.

The business plan or road map outlines your business for the short term, which could be 3-5 years or longer, not recommend going past five years because the world of business changes, what seems to be daily.

There are nine key parts to writing a business plan and it all starts with the executive summary. What's this executive summary you may ask?

The executive summary is like looking through to what you anticipate your business future to be, a glimpse of you will of your business. This is one of the biggest challenges that new business owners face when starting a new business because of terminology. For example, mission statement, basic company information, product (s), the potential for growth, etc.

When we look harder at what our mission statement is or should be, we need not to confuse our mission statement with what our vision is. The mission statement is something that you will use to outline the goals of your business and it's something that you will work to achieve over the next 3-5 years. Whereas our vision statement is something that we would like to see our business over a period of time, again you'll put the work in but you may have to adjust your time line on your vision statement.

When writing your business plan, make sure that every word, every detail counts, after all this is just another tool to help you succeed. You should also keep your business plan clean, clear, concise, and easy to read and understand.

Why the mission statement is key to your business's success? This will be your first opportunity to wow new investors and obtain funding. You should also limit your mission statement to roughly about a paragraph and try to hook your reader quickly.

Once you're satisfied with your mission statement you will need to write a brief summary about the company. Company information gives you a chance to showcase either the knowledge you've gained from working in this field and/or your expertise in this field through education. This section is where you get to introduce yourself and the other key members of the decision-making process in your business.

The company section gives you a chance to explain to new investors where your business is located, what role you're going to have in the company, how many employees there are/or will be needed to achieve your short-term goals. This is also an opportunity to give when your business was founded, what is corporate status and be sure to give details on every founder or decision maker highlighting their experience and expertise and why they play an important role in your company's success.

While the mission statement and company information are only tidbits of information about your business, it is when you begin to talk about your company's growth, financial abilities, and your product (s) or services you get the ability to shine.

However, if you're a new business or a startup and your goal is to obtain funding to open the doors of your business then you're not going to have growth or a profit/loss to highlight. How do you overcome this hurtle when you have limited to no information to give?

Well if we start with your company's growth or potential growth, we must first understand the market we are trying to break into. After you've researched companies that are offering the same product (s) or services, you can chart out their highs and lows for a quarter. This is where the use of visual aids and can really help you Excel on selling your idea. The use of charts using what would potentially be a competitor can help you sell your reasoning why the market can afford another with limited loss and maximum gain. How is this done?

This process is used on the hypothesis level, "the X company as seen an upward shift in sales and yet they're not utilizing growth potential to move past the metro area."

"My company, company A has disciplined founders that have worked or educated themselves in business development; if we move outward using the same Consumer targets, company A should either mirror the success of company X or surpass company X's goals."

This type of charting can help you sell the idea that you can operate your business on the same level as the upper level management of company X.

Using the same concept as above can also help you highlight why your product (s) and or services can drive your revenue potential up. Highlighting your product (s) or services gives you a chance to do a multitude of things within this portion of the business plan. You can for example, show how your product (s) or services can set you and your potential competition apart, it can also showcase your ability to compete on a larger scope.

We must remember that as new business owners that were under the gun so to speak more so than an established business. New business owners have the burden to prove to investors that their idea is a tangible, legitimate, and obtainable idea. The goal of briefly describing your product (s) or services is nothing more than a sales pitch, with variables from every angle on the reason why you either shouldn't take that step or it's been done before and market analysis don't see the potential for a company of the same nature.

However, I've said it before and will continue to reiterate this as my opinion only, if you believe in your business model, product (s) or services, and the people that gave you the building blocks to get to this point; you must always use market share research as your go to guide for your next move.

One of your most important steps in a new business is creditability, creditworthiness, and your bank information. Yes...We've hit the dreaded financial part of your business plan. It is at this point where you'll learn a word that you've hated since your childhood, no! This will be your answer for new business owners, it's like the test word; I'll tell him no today but I'm going to approve him in 30-60 days from now. If you've written your business plan for financial funding you will soon understand, that is unless you have that perfect partner, brother, sister, whatever.

I'm a firm believer that everyone gets their finding denied on the first try simply because the lending institutions want to see how bad do you really want to be your own boss, are ready for that type of responsibility, and they just really didn't like the execution of your business plan. When it comes to funding for your business it's important that you don't get discouraged if you're turned down on the first submission of your business plan. There are many lenders out there who are willing to take a risk on a new business; some you will find at the small business administration; the SBA alone can lead you in the right direction for your funding needs of your new business.

 The last and finial part of what you should hope to have as a well-organized business plan is a summary. Most often people new to business plans and the business world confuse this summary with a conclusion, to close out your business plan. The fact is that your business plan is a living breathing entity all in its self or at least metaphorically, that's what it's considered. The summary of your business plan is nothing more that a vision statement. Where would you like to see your business in the short term and the long term, how do you plan to get it there, what avenues will you have available to you to obtain the growth that you feel needed to be successful in your market.

EXAMPLE CHARTS FOR COMPANY A AND X

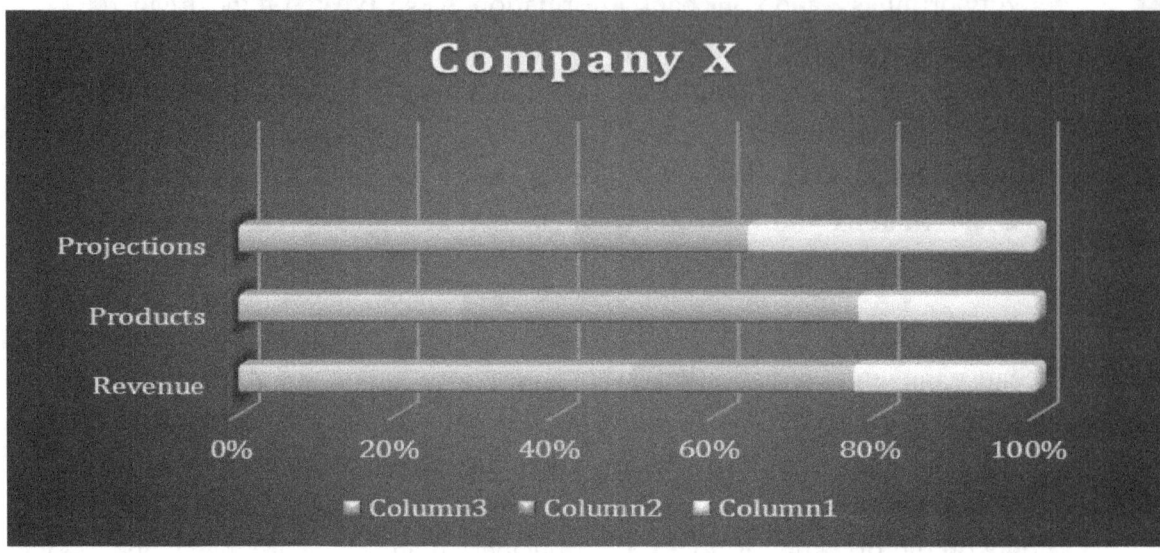

Basics of Business

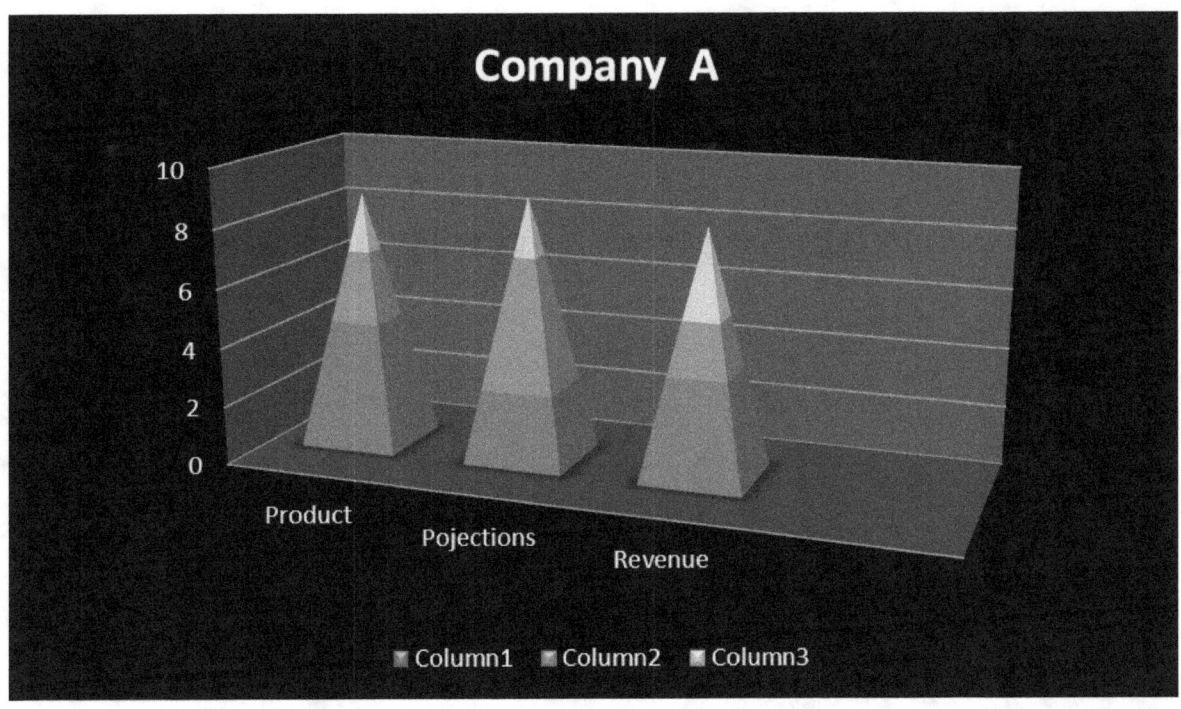

Chapter Four

Business Ethics/Social Responsibility

How do business ethics apply in today's digital world? Business ethics affect many different scenarios in the workplace. For example, business ethics protect employees from a hostile work environment, provides training for employees, and it impacts sales, marketing and your businesses social responsibility. The biggest question when business ethics are mentioned is how we can as employers serve our employees better, fact remains no matter the size of your business there will be at least one employee at some point in your businesses future.

While business ethics cannot measure a business owner only on business ethics alone; due to the fact that a business owner must take into account their social responsibility. However, if the business owner tries to take to many short cuts, it could damage employee morale and leave the business owner shorthanded but also open to legal issues; if at any time the employee were to make accusations about the work environment.

Ethics is something that is almost always instilled in us early on as children. While business ethics is a direct correlation with business policy, it's still understanding right from wrong.

When dealing with business ethics you may find yourself lost in a variety of situations but the fact remains that as children we're taught right from wrong, otherwise the conscience may be severe.

Well much like us in a child state business ethics are dealt with in a similar fashion only on a different platform. For example, while it is important from an ethical standpoint to provide proper training for employees, failure to do this can lead you to a long line of ethical dilemmas.

A business owner's responsibility is to provide a safe work environment, understanding that discrimination of race, sex, or religion is not only a violation of the law but an example of poor business ethical policies. While one may not have anything to do with the other, so you may think; the evaluation of hiring employees or how your human resources department picks its applicants may cause an ethical dilemma for you and your business.

Practicing good business ethics or bad business ethics can ultimately affect your profit/loss margin in your market. Some key points to consider are sales, marketing, and how you pick and choose your outside vendors to maintain your supply and demand.

These are some key factors that could alter how your business is perceived, if your business ethics policies are not monitored and in enforced. Another example of poor business ethics is how you choose your vendors; if you've chosen friends or family to maintain your supply and demand over a vendor that is more qualified or has a better price point, you in danger your business, your employee's income source, as well as economic structure and growth.

While we may end up in a position to help our friends and family through the development of our business, it is the larger scope of our business that we have to look at. The reality of it is we didn't go into business to solidify friendships and family relationships. You've strived to open the doors of your business whether virtually or physically to obtain a goal.

Those goals whether long term or short term work in conjunction with your business's success. The practice of failed business ethics can be eradicated at the earliest stages of your business's development. However, the consciences of using unethical business practices will have a direct effect on the community that you serve, this directly affect your community's economy as well as your business growth. This is most commonly known as a business's social responsibility.

This type of scenario goes far beyond the scope of how ethics are really seen in today's world of business. Most consider ethics from a legal point of view and others argue that it goes beyond the basic right and wrong training we take on as children and then when we enter the college classroom. However, the vetting process you use to determine the future of your business hinders on a multitude of variables. For example, you can hire what is perceived to be the perfect employee; that is until a major rift occurs in that employee's home life. The first and foremost is to always communicate the importance of the ethical policies you've instilled in your business. Training the employee to understand the importance of practicing good business ethics can lead that employee to your office door if that rift starts to show in their work ethic.

It's important to understand that employees may not be as devoted to making your business first priority. How does this play a role in questionable ethics? First, you have to remember that you to were at the mercy of a business owner before moving to the business owner's shoes, understanding signs of unrest in your employees are key to solving the bigger dilemma.

When did employee, morale go down, what's the cause and effect of the low morale, and how's this going to affect your business in both the short term and long term? Utilizing a set of your own business ethics you'll find that employee morale is one if not the most important variable in your businesses success.

Examining the three questions from above has identifiers, if the morale of your employees dropped because you've hired a family member or friend to lead your employees, after some have been with you from the beginning; this is most likely your identifier and an example of unethical business practices.

However, if the employee you've chosen to lead the rest of your employees, has become abrasive or has been abrasive without your knowledge, moving that employee out of the authoritative position could raise employee morale, as well as this could be another identifier of a major conflict in his/her home life; having an open-door policy shows your employees that they are able to voice their concerns without reprisal.

Although, this may solve your issue with the employee morale, as business owners we must remember that like being a practitioner of good business ethics, we also have a social and economic responsibility. This scenario serves as a premier example of the "not my problem," if the business owner does nothing about the employee, whom he thought was trained enough to lead. The larger scope shows us that business owners who treat their employees as just a worker will most likely face some sort of unrest from his/her workforce.

The business ethical policies alone are not able to solve this problem, with the correlation of business ethics and social responsibility, the employee will be able to maintain his income, employee morale will rise, the devotional effort from the business owner will show trustworthiness, and employees will want to maintain longevity.

When social responsibility is called into question, some of the key components are asked, how does business ethics and social responsibility work hand in hand?

In it's very definition social responsibility and business ethics are the implementation of ethics and morals, but as a society how do they impact our way of life? Although, the small business may not have certain ethical policies and codes of conduct that larger institutions have. The small business owner unknowingly has a certain code, ethics, and laws that they either live by or are forced to maintain due to legal regulations.

Basics of Business

Chapter Five

Choosing the structure that's right for your business

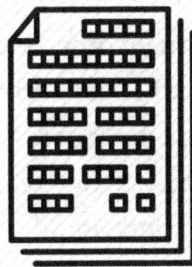 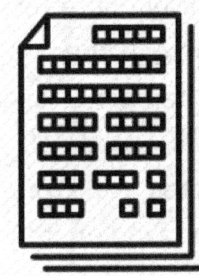 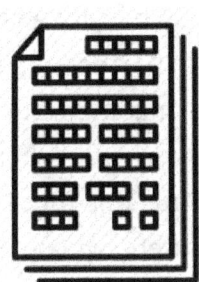

One of the most important decisions you will have to make before taking your business idea to the next level is its structure. The legal form or structures are (sole proprietorship, corporation, limited liability company, etc.) this will be a key fundamental step in how you operate your business, tax breaks, and how you can protect your personal assets. The legal structure of your business will also help you evaluate how you proceed with your business in the future, some of the variables are starting your business as a sole proprietor and evolving into a limited liability company, S-corporation or a C-corporation, which have their own set of taxes, tax schedules, tax liabilities, and tax breaks and cuts for new and small business owners. Some of these variables that deal with your corporate status will allow to change your status for new partners, investors as your business experiences growth within the market. Other key factors that should influence your decision on your new business corporate structure are the protection of your personal assets but you should weigh the pros and cons of every corporate structure and pick the best structure that fits your new business.

- **Sole proprietorship/self-employed-** The business and the owner are legally the same. From the IRS's perspective, the business is not a taxable entity. Instead, all of the business assets and liabilities and income are treated as belonging directly to the business owner.

- **General partnership and/or LLP**- As with sole proprietorships, the business and the owners (two or more) are legally the same. A partnership is not a taxable entity under federal law. There is no separate partnership income tax, as there is a corporate income tax. Instead, income from the partnership is taxed to the individual partners, at their own individual tax rates. For tax purposes, all of the income of the partnership must be reported as distributed or "passed-through" to the partners, who will then be taxed on it through their individual returns.

- **Limited liability Company** (LLC). Under state laws, LLC owners are given the liability protection that was previously afforded only to owners of a corporation (shareholders). Now, LLCs are treated like partnerships for federal tax purposes (unless they elect to be treated like a corporation, which most don't). LLCs have "pass-through" taxation, which means that no tax on the LLC's income is paid at the business level. Income/loss is instead reported on the personal tax returns of the owners and any tax due is paid at the individual level, Keep in mind; even though LLCs are treated as partnerships for federal tax purposes, the same is not always true for state tax purposes.

- **C -Corporation**- The C Corporation, also called the "regular" corporation, is subject to corporate income tax. Income earned by a C corporation is normally taxed at the corporate level using the corporate income tax rates. C corporation income is also subject to what is called "double taxation," when the income of the business is distributed to the owners in the form of dividends, because dividends are taxable. Tax is paid first by the corporation on its income and then again by the owners on the dividends received. If the owner draws a salary from the corporation, that salary is also subject to income tax withholding such as, Medicare, social security, state and local, plus federal taxation.

- **S corporation**- The S Corporation is a corporation that has filed a special election with the IRS to be treated like a partnership (or LLC) for tax purposes. Therefore, S corporations are not subject to corporate income tax. Instead, their income is subject to what is often called "pass-through" taxation, where the income or loss of the business is passed through the company to the owners (shareholders). Having pass-through taxation means that S corporation income is not subject to double taxation like C corporation income.

This is a default table that will help you understand the variables of choosing the right corporate structure that meets your needs and your business needs. However, the most popular corporate structure is the L.L.C or L.L.P because it is the protection of your personal assets and any partners that have joined your business.

Common taxes that you may need to take into consideration are listed below. However, laws for many states may differ and this table should be used as a guide and not an absolute.

- ❖ **Income tax-** Income tax can be classified as either corporate income tax or individual income tax. For those business types that pass-through business income to the individual owners, individual income tax is paid.
- ❖ **Corporate tax-** This is a tax imposed on corporations, limited liability companies (LLCs) and other business types formed by a

state-filing for the mere privilege of being incorporated in that state.
- ❖ **Sales tax**- There are different types of sales taxes and some are paid by the seller while others are paid by the buyer.
- ❖ **Property tax**- Most property taxes is used to fund local governments versus state government, but should also be considered as a tax obligation your business will incur. Owning real estate is not a requirement for you start your business but you may have to pay property tax if you've invested some of your business capital into a brick and mortar store front, office, and /or warehouse.

Business income and appropriate deductions on behalf of your business:

When it comes to determining your business's income tax it is highly recommended to retain an accountant and to maintain some type of accountant software. While it's important to remember that accounts should be the one to help manage your tax obligations, keeping a detailed account of your profits, business expense, and subtracting the cost of your service or goods, gives you your business income. However, when there is any type of income directly connected to your business, this will be equated and added to your overall business income and will be required to pay taxes on it, no matter what your corporate status is.

Gross income from sales- In most cases, this will be the bulk of the income you receive from actually operating your business.

Miscellaneous business income- The miscellaneous portion of your business income can range from a variety of options and if not properly trained with the current tax year laws and regulation could result in either paying too much in taxes or too little on behalf of your business. While taxes on an individual level can get complicated, for example, if you've employed 1099 employees and fail to report correctly, this could lead to serious deficiency in your businesses annual report that you must file showing the company's profit/loss with your state department of revenue, secretary of state, and or the internal revenue service. Although, business income has many different categories to take in to consideration when filling your business income taxes, there are a number of different business-related types of income must be reported on your tax return.

Deductions- being a new business owner that has the daunting task of figuring out deductions on your first-year business income or personal wage from your new business can become complicated if you don't fully understand the current tax laws and regulations. It's to your best interest to either use a tax specialist or if you must go at alone obtain proven tax software, this will give you the option of reading a list of deductions that may apply to you. You as a business owner should make sure that your deductions are legitimate; this will help you achieve your goal to a lower tax amount owed.

Self-employment/sole proprietor taxes- sole proprietors, your net business income is the amount on which you must pay self-employment taxes of course like everything else in business other than federal guide lines, the bracketed amount you pay to the federal government maybe higher or lower considering the state in which your business is located. While in the previous table, there is a list of different types of entities you can choose from to form your business, ultimately you're looking for the corporate status that will best suit your business needs; therefore, the rules for self-employed/ sole-proprietors, s-corporation, c-corporation, and LLC are all different and are held on different tax bracts.

Net operating gain/ losses- Owning your first business can be somewhat overwhelming and no learning curves provided. It is up to you at this point to be able to understand certain concepts in business; especially dealing with the IRS because they're not going to grant you any favors for the "I didn't know clause." With that being said realistic business person will understand that most likely you will be able to obtain a fair wage for the work you do at your business; however, you will most likely operate in the negative for the first two to five years.

```
Gross Profit  =  Net Sales   −   Cost of Goods Sold
Gross Profit  =  $100,000    −   $75,000
Gross Profit  =  $25,000
```

Claiming tax credits

Beyond tax deductions, minimize your income tax bill by claiming tax credits—they are generally preferable because they're subtracted directly from your tax bill. Deductions, in contrast, are subtracted from the income on which your tax bill is based. As great as tax credits can be, they are only available for certain situations or industries (e.g., research and development, home-buying, car buying, or alternative energy production). And credits come with a set of very complicated rules, which you or your tax pro must follow in order to claim.

Dealing with the IRS

As a small business owner, be aware of your tax payment obligations and when they are due—even if you use a tax adviser or accountant. There's no worse feeling than watching your cash surplus disappear because of an impending IRS payment. Worse yet is discovering that funds have been spent elsewhere because you didn't realize a tax payment was due. With a good awareness of your filing and payment obligations, you can avoid unexpected payments or penalties.

Chapter Six

Selecting Business Insurance

What are the policy types?

There are different types of business insurance that provide different types of coverage. There's coverage against damages to your business's location (office, factory, etc.), vehicles, and equipment and inventory. There's business insurance to protect against losses resulting from crimes, such as theft or even employee fraud. There are many types of business liability insurance, protecting your company in the event of a lawsuit. There is also business insurance to provide coverage for extended leaves of absence due to illness.

What are the general categories?

Business insurance can be divided into four broad categories:

Business property insurance: Reimburses any insured party who has suffered a financial loss because property (land, buildings, personal property, etc.) has been damaged or destroyed. Business liability insurance, delivers protection to pay for bodily injury or property damages when the insured is legally responsible.

Business automobile insurance:

Provides protection against damages caused by employees that may be involved in an automobile accident, these vehicles primary function are for business use. Similar to personal automobile insurance, comprehensive coverage provides compensation for vehicle damages resulting from fire or theft; collision covers losses due to an accident; and liability coverage protects you if you are sued for an accident involving a company vehicle. Obtaining simple business umbrella insurance policy Extends coverage for losses above the limit of other policies. An umbrella policy may also extend coverage for losses not normally covered in the other policy. Outside of these four primary categories, other types of business insurance coverage include: worker's compensation insurance, business interruption insurance, group health insurance, group life insurance and disability insurance.

Choosing the right limits and deductibles

Once you select the right type of coverage for your business, you'll also need to choose the appropriate limits and deductibles to suit your needs. These factors can greatly influence the premiums you pay:

Get the best coverage at the best price. Obtain and compare multiple quotes from reputable carriers and independent insurance agents. You can get quotes online or in person. If you are a member of an industry organization, check to see if they have a recommended insurance provider. It's also often beneficial to talk to other business owners to see who provides their insurance and whether they're satisfied.

Compare the details in Policies from different carriers; however, may have the same name, but not the same coverage. Clarity on what is and is not covered in each policy should be a consideration in relation to your premium. However, the same Considerations for home-based businesses and Owners of small home-based businesses can often add a rider to their homeowner's policy instead of needing a separate business insurance policy. Discuss your situation with an insurance agent to determine what is best for you.

Understanding common elements and exclusions

Before deciding the type of coverage for your business, be sure you know what various policies will cover.

> **Endorsements-** Specialized coverage types are more restricted in scope and cover situations excluded in a comprehensive general liability insurance policy. Sometimes you can pay an additional premium for an "endorsement"—an amendment to a comprehensive that will cover a standard exclusion. When liability relates to a unique risk (e.g., professional services by an accountant), a specialized policy will be required (e.g., an errors and omissions or E&O policy), in addition to a comprehensive general liability insurance policy.

Coverage of occurrences- A comprehensive policy covers liability for any "occurrence" during the period—that is, the policy will cover liability for personal injuries or property damage that the insured caused to another party while the policy was in effect. A lapse in insurance coverage opens a window of vulnerability.

Expected or intended damages- Damages that were subjectively "expected or intended" by the insured are excluded from coverage. Courts have ruled that to deny a claim, it is not sufficient for the insurance company to prove that a "reasonable person" would have expected the outcome. Rather, the insurance company must prove what the insured party was actually thinking at the time, which is a tall order to meet.

Intellectual property, advertising, etc.: Coverage for personal injuries to other persons as a result of libel; slander; defamation; invasion of privacy; copyright, patent, trade name and trademark infringement; and unfair business practices--traditionally has been included in a comprehensive policy. Recently, however, insurance companies have added exclusions from coverage for copyright, patent, trade name and trademark infringement. They are also narrowly defining "advertising," to limit or deny coverage. Be sure to examine any proposed comprehensive general liability policy for this type of coverage.

Data as property- Coverage for damages to another person's property only may apply if the property is "tangible," or the damage "physical." It's up for debate as to whether computer data is "tangible," or capable of "physical" harm. So, if you provide computer hardware, software, or programming services, make you aware of what your policy covers.

Property Insurance Distinguished- A single policy may provide for comprehensive general liability coverage (for damages caused to other persons in the form of personal injuries and property loss) and separate coverage for damage to property owned by the insured. Remember that comprehensive general liability coverage alone does not offer protection for damage to property owned by the insured. Property insurance must be included in the policy for the insured's property to be covered.

Basics of Business

Chapter Seven

Marketing

Marketing consist of multiple activities happening at once, while, at Colorado Technical University undertaking my Associates degree in business learning about marketing was a fundamental step to business success. However, if you breakdown the beginning pieces to the puzzle of marketing from your college years or maybe you didn't go to college and yourself taught, you've most likely heard of the four P's. What exactly is the four P's, you might be asking yourself? The four P's are the key fundament placement of a well-organized marketing strategy for any business, whether new or old. Every business owner has taken into account their: Product, Place, Promotion, and Price.

The four P's are only the starting point to an effective marketing strategy and in this digital age most everyone considers the only marketing that's effective is digital. Unfortunatly if this is your thought process let's go ahead and evaluate a consumer base that uses a tablet but finds themselves traveling for their employer the majority of the time and how do the lack of smell, touch, and actually handling the product in your possession effect the consumer?

The digital age we live in gives us the ability to pick and choose from a varity of different vendors and if we're a vendor than this works to our advantage but what about traditional marketing? What about the person traveling in their automobile, first evaluate how they purchased or rented their automobile, booked their train, plane, or bus tickets? Most likely a digital platform was used to make their temporary booking purchases but is there enough consumer confidence in today's digital e-commerce arena to spend a large amount of money, reaching into the thousands online if you are not a vendor purchasing your inventory from wholesalers that you've spent time developing a repor with?

While buying books, clothes, and shoes may seem like the likely commerce for online shoppers of today, they were lead to those very specific landing pages, shopping carts, billboards, and coffee shops from the marketing stragey behind the scenes. If thinking that online marketing is the online platform needed to compete in your market you may be right if the market you're trying to break in to is strictly online shopper's bonanza. However, the effectives of auto wraps, mobile billboards, billboards, newspaper ads, are still very much used today. The question is how to use them effectively and why most marketers don't want you to use them?

The examination of the print ad has still remained strong because simply computers crash but you may want to reach a very generalized geo-target area which is plausible with online marketing, that is in a month or so. The fact remains that you can purchase billboard space for a month or more, run a magazine ad, newspaper ad, flyers, etc. and begin obtaining the exposure you're looking for within a week; while, google, Bing, yahoo, and other search engines can take in the upwards of a month or more.

The reasoning behind an effective marketing stragey is not to break the bank in so many words but garner exposure quickly and let the marketing strategy pay for itself. The new business owner as well as one that has a time tested proven business model should have one common goal in mind dealing with all facets of their business and that's that your business should be self-sufficient. When you start recruiting a marketing firm remember that whether you do it online or through the yellow pages, the digital era has provided us with a multitude of choices and you interview each firm, as if they are your future employee; it's essential that you understand the line that you're drawing when taking the step of business owner; you and you alone should be impartial and make the choice for your business that's going to provide the best revenue generator.

Marketing and understanding how to price your product in a competitive market can be tricky if you've not done a proper market analysis work up. For example, randomly choosing a price just because it sounds goods is not using the tools that are readily available to you, to come up with a competitive price, you must first examine the product as a whole. Once you've done this, you will need to breakdown the product into production variables. For example, how much did it cost to produce the product, ship the product, package the product, and handle the product? These numbers can help you as a starting point for a stage of marketing.

The next step to this breakdown is the evaltion of your store front; do you have a brick and mortar store, are you online only, is your office in your home or are you paying for office space, electrical, water, and staff? These variables give you a guide line to attempt to come up with a price point. Every facet of your business needs to be equated into the price per unit of your product, down to the single price per product. Much like everything else in life there is a mathematical formula to help you come up with your price per unit, per product to attempt to operate in the positive.

Unfortunately, you can quickly price yourself out of your market by having your prices to high. So, how do you overcome this? Marketing and having a solidified customer base though marketing. Obviously, the quickest way to market yourself is going to be on a digital platform because let's face it who doesn't have a smart phone or tablet? It is the placement of your marketing that gives you the best result as well as the geo-targeting that can help you succeed in your business field. A perfect example is Google AdWords, this service gives you the funanality to pick exact locations, keywords, create specific ads that will draw your customers to your web address. This is just one of many ways to begin a marketing plan for a new small business.

Once you've come with a competitive price point, a geographical target, a product/ or service, and a budget able promotion plan; it's time to consider branding. Branding is more in depth than just coming up with a product name or business name. This is when your product, promotion, geo-target, price, your business name, and your product's creditworthiness stand on its own. A good example of branding is a marketing platform that google owns google AdWords; this is a product that was created by google the company, promoted by google, given a price point by google, and it now stands on its own. This example can be used as a goal to reach in the long term but understanding that the same tools of branding apply for your product.

Chapter Eight

Financial processing

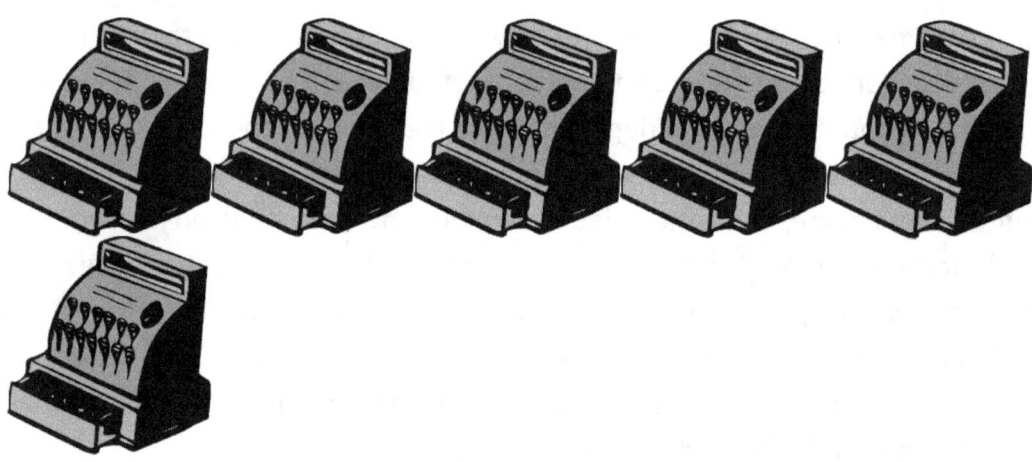

Accepting Cash Only

Cash is the most commonly accepted and reliable form of payment for a business. Many small businesses operate as "cash only" merchants. Years ago, this wouldn't have been uncommon, but with advances in technology, business owners must ask themselves if they're hurting their bottom line by limiting payment options.

If you're thinking about starting a cash only business or if you're considering expanding your current payment options, be aware of the pros and cons of only accepting cash.

Pros of accepting only cash:

Cash payments ensure that businesses receive funds immediately. With each transaction, your business immediately receives the appropriate payment amount without the worry of waiting periods or not getting paid at all.

Cash is the simplest form of payment and therefore involves less bookkeeping. For a business, that not only means less stress and hassle, but it also may save money in the time and labor it would take for a bookkeeper to record other payments methods.

There is limited risk of fraud when accepting cash only. There are cases of counterfeit cash payments, but compared to other payment methods, fraud is much less common in cash transactions.

Cash only businesses don't have to worry about third parties or fees associated with other payment options.

Cons of accepting only cash:

Customers who do not have enough cash on them will have to walk away from a purchase they would otherwise make.

Your business may lose customers by only accepting cash. As card payments become more and more popular, many consumers expect this to be an option when making purchases. If they find that a particular business only accepts cash, they may feel inconvenienced and shop elsewhere.

Keeping large sums of cash on your business's premises increases the amount of time you'll spend managing finances and also creates an added security risk.

The IRS requires that you file a Form 8300 if your business receives more than $10,000 in cash from one buyer as a result of a single transaction or two or more related transactions. The same rule applies to cash equivalents such as traveler's checks, bank drafts, cashier's checks, and money orders. The form requires the name, address, and Social Security number of the buyer.

The nature of some small businesses may make it smarter to stay cash only. Flea markets, street vendors, and lawn service providers are just a few examples of common cash only small businesses. At the end of the day, you will have to decide which payment options will create the most success for your business.

Accepting Checks:

Although credit and debit card payments are on the rise, the expenses and additional record-keeping involved with card payments are not ideal for all businesses. If you want to expand your customer payment options beyond cash but aren't ready to make the leap to card payments, accepting checks is another option to consider.

To protect the financial health of your business, understand the laws that regulate check payment policies.

Policies for Accepting Checks

If your business accepts personal checks, establish a detailed check acceptance policy to help identify and avoid bad checks. Don't just make a document and file it away--be sure to train your employees on the new policies and post reminders in visible and prominent locations.

Common check policies include variations of these guidelines:

Checks must be from a local or in-state bank

Checks should not be written and accepted for more than the purchase amount

Checks should not be accepted that are starter checks, unnumbered checks, or non-personalized checks

Accepted checks should be deposited as quickly as possible. Banks may refuse to honor checks dated back six months or more

- ❖ Instruct your employees to carefully examine every personal check for information that is essential for cashing the check:

- ❖ Personalization - The customer's complete name and address must appear on the check

- ❖ Date - The check date must be current. Do not accept post- or future-dated checks

Bank I.D. numbers - The check must have a bank identification number, or routing transit number, that runs across the bottom, along with the customer's account number and check number. This information is used by a bank to identify the transaction and resolve payment issues

- ❖ Payee - The "Pay to the Order of" section must indicate your business's name

- ❖ Dollar amounts - Both the written and numeric amounts must match

- ❖ Customer Signature - The check should be signed in your presence and verified with photo identification

Verifying:

Verifying identification can help your business safeguard against fraud. However, some state laws regulate which forms of identification businesses can require to see. Depending on your business location, it may be illegal to require customers to show a credit card as a condition for accepting their check. Commonly accepted forms of identification often include a state-issued driver's license, I.D. card, or military I.D.

Follow these tips when verifying customer identification:

Make sure the signature on the customer's identification matches the signature on the customer's check

Use discretion when recording personal information like phone numbers, identification numbers and expiration dates

Trust your instincts and be on the lookout for suspicious behavior or fraud "red flags." For questionable transactions, call the customer's bank to verify legitimacy of a check

Bounced Checks:

What should you do if a check is returned because a customer's account is closed, or has insufficient funds to pay for the transaction? In addition to instituting a check policy, some new businesses are employing the help of electronic check verification companies to identify flagged individuals. For a monthly fee, businesses can compare a customer's name against a database of individuals that are known to have written bad, stolen or forged checks.

Even with precautionary measures in place, businesses that accept checks may still have a bad check occasionally slip by. If a check fails to clear on your first attempt, your bank will generally attempt a second deposit. In some cases, the customer can quickly resolve the problem by transferring or depositing funds to cover a bounced check. If the issue is not resolved by the customer, you can consult your local law enforcement agency to understand your rights and options. Some states require businesses to mail a registered letter and allow a designated waiting period to lapse before further action is taken.

If the issue remains unresolved, consider filing a suit with a small claims court or employing a collection agency to resolve the payment. Many businesses choose to employ a collection agency to avoid a lengthy and expensive court settlement.

Dissatisfied Customers:

Occasionally, you'll find a customer has stopped payment on a check if they believe the products or services bought did not live up to expectations. If this is true, customers may be entitled to a refund or a reduction of the amount owed.

Accepting Credit Cards:

Credit and debit cards are popular, convenient, flexible, and have become increasingly important in business commerce. If your business is considering what forms of payment to accept, or if you'd like to expand the payment options of your cash-only business, be sure to go over the pros and cons of accepting card payments.

Pros of Accepting Card Payments:

Card payments are evolving into the most common method of customer payment.

Businesses can easily accept card payments.

The convenience of using credit cards generally increases the likelihood of consumer "impulse purchases," which ultimately contributes to an increase in a business's average sale. Customers are more likely to make these purchases if they have access to credit or their available bank account funds.

Cons of Accepting Card Payments:

Card payments come with an increased risk of fraud. Although there are laws and security measures that help protect and secure customer information, card payments are inherently more susceptible to foul play than cash. Read more about your responsibilities to protect your customers' privacy and secure their personal information.

Businesses that accept card payments encounter small processing fees for purchase transactions. These fees seem insignificant but they can certainly add up, especially if your business accepts a lot of small purchases on credit cards. Setting up the necessary equipment to accept cards also carries additional costs.

Card transactions add another layer of detail to your business's bookkeeping practices. Your business will have to take into account the additional time and resources it takes to maintain these records.

The Bottom Line:

Accepting card payments will, at least initially, cost your business money and add extra processes in your daily operations. Many small business owners look at this as a necessary operating expense. As card payments become more popular, customers will likely begin to expect a plastic option as a rule, rather than a courtesy.

Online Payment Services:

Online payment services allow business and consumers to exchange money electronically over the Internet. With an online payment service, your business can receive payment from virtually any customer with an email account. Online payment services have recently become very popular with businesses and consumers.

Advantages of Online Payment Services:

Online payment services can either replace or supplement your decision to accept credit and debit cards. Opening an online payment account is often faster and easier than setting up a Merchant Account (which is required to accept credit and debit card payments). Online payment accounts typically incur smaller fees than a traditional Merchant Account, which can have a big impact on businesses with many small transactions. From a customer-service perspective, it's beneficial to have multiple payment options available. Online payment services are also user-friendly and can simplify the payment process by storing customer card information or billing customers at a later date.

Disadvantages of Online Payment Services

As with all payment methods, online payment services have their drawbacks. Most of these services redirect customers to a payment service website to complete a transaction. Being forced to leave your business's website can be confusing for customers - especially those new to online shopping - and could make them abandon a purchase they may have otherwise made.

Your business may not get enough value out of offering both an online payment service and accepting card payments. On the other hand, limited payment options may turn some customers away. Finding the right balance of payment options is something that is unique for every business.

Security Concerns

Major providers of online payment services have developed features like two-factor authentication to help businesses enhance e-commerce security. Two-factor authentication requires businesses to enter a six-digit code in addition to their password, making third-party scams rare. As e-commerce becomes more popular, security features will continue to evolve. Be sure to research service provider plans for the most current security technology.

Shopping Cart Services

Online payment services require a virtual shopping cart. Virtual shopping carts allow businesses to accept orders on multiple products from their website. A shopping cart can calculate the total, tax, and shipping costs of an order, in addition to collecting customer account and shipping information.

Some online payment service providers offer free shopping cart services to businesses. If your online payment service does not provide a free, secure shopping cart option, third-party shopping cart services can be used.

Extending Credit to Your Customers

By extending credit to your customers, you give them the option to purchase products or services today and pay for them at a later date. When your business accepts credit card payments and personal checks or invoices customers, it is essentially extending credit on the assumption that customers have the funds to pay for the transaction.

When you extend credit to customers through card payments, the credit card company manages the risk. When you extend credit through invoices or personal checks, you are responsible for verifying and accepting payments and managing the risks that come with them.

Extending credit through invoices is common in some industries such as construction or manufacturing, but may not be practical for every business. To decide if extending credit is right for your business, weigh the associated rewards and risks.

The option of credit enables customers to focus less on prices, enhances customer relations, and has the potential to generate more sales.

Extending credit costs money. When you sell something on credit, you will not have payment on hand and will need to temporarily recoup the cost from other areas of your operating capital.

If customers don't pay, you could be in for a long settlement process that may not end in your favor.

Ask yourself if you have a significant business need to extend credit. Extending credit could be the factor that keeps your business afloat if it makes it easier for your customers to buy from you. Nevertheless, if it isn't necessary it may not be worth the extra time and paperwork.

Establish Credit Practices

Before you extend credit to customers, be sure to establish detailed policies and understand consumer protection laws.

Determine to whom you will extend credit such as individual customers or other businesses. Run credit checks on all customers before you agree to extend credit.

Develop clear, consistent payment guidelines. Your bills should indicate when payment is due, when it will be considered delinquent, and who to contact with questions.

Determine how you will bill or invoice customers. Will you or your employees mail requests for payment yourselves, or will you hire another company to handle invoicing?

Create a plan for collecting late or defaulted payments. Regardless of the type of application or documents you use for credit transactions, be sure to get all of your customers' information in writing. In return, provide them with a copy of your payment policy, which spells out how penalties will be applied to late payments and how you will handle unpaid bills. It's important to have this documentation in case a fraudulent or delinquent credit transaction occurs.

Comply with Consumer Credit Laws

If your business extends credit to customers, you should become aware of consumer credit laws. The Federal Trade Commission (FTC) enforces the nation's consumer protection laws. These laws regulate how you advertise interest rates, how much time you have to respond to billing-mistake claims, how aggressive you can be when attempting to collect a debt, and other aspects of extending credit and debt collections.

Dealing with Bankrupt Customers and Collecting Debt:

What happens when a customer refuses to pay a bill? When you've gone beyond adding late penalties and you still haven't seen any payment, check with your local consumer protection agency to understand your options and state laws. This information will help you decide if you should report these actions to the police, employ a collection agency, or attempt to settle the payment by other means. Depending on your local laws and the severity of the delinquent transactions, it may be cheaper to simply swallow the debt.

You may find yourself in a situation where a customer to whom you've extended credit declares bankruptcy. In this instance, the debtor then has the benefit of an automatic stay immediately upon filing a bankruptcy petition. This stay stops you from taking any further action of trying to collect the debt unless or until the bankruptcy court decides otherwise.

If a money judgment is awarded to you in court, further action may still be needed to receive payment. Such action may include contacting the defendant, or in some cases, providing information about the defendant to a law enforcement officer so that they can assist you in collecting the debt.

The best way to solve these situations is by preventing them from happening through strict credit policies and by conducting appropriate evaluations of credit risks before extending any credit.

Mechanics' Liens:

Mechanics' and materialmen's liens have specific regulations that apply to their industries in cases where credited customers fail to make their payments. Liens exist in most states to provide special collection rights to those who provide services or building materials used to improve real property. If the debt is not paid, the lien can be foreclosed and the property sold to pay the obligation. For more information on the specific laws that govern these debts, visit your state's Department of Consumer Affairs or Protection.

Chapter Nine

Business Funding

7(a) Loan Program Eligibility

The requirements of eligibility for the 7(a)-loan program are based on specific aspects of the business and its principals. As such, the key factors of eligibility are based on what the business does to receive its income, the character of its ownership and where the business operates.

SBA generally does not specify what businesses are eligible. Rather, the agency outlines what businesses are not eligible. However, there are some universally applicable requirements. To be eligible for assistance, businesses must:

- Operate for profit
- Be small, as defined by SBA
- Be engaged in, or propose to do business in, the United States or its possessions
- Have reasonable invested equity
- Use alternative financial resources, including personal assets, before seeking financial assistance
- Be able to demonstrate a need for the loan proceeds
- Use the funds for a sound business purpose
- Not be delinquent on any existing debt obligations to the U.S. government
- Ineligible Businesses

A business must be engaged in an activity SBA determines as acceptable for financial assistance from a federal provider. The following types of businesses are not eligible for assistance

because of the activities they conduct:

Financial businesses primarily engaged in the business of lending, such as banks, finance companies, payday lenders, some leasing companies and factors (pawn shops, although engaged in lending, may qualify in some circumstances)

Businesses owned by developers and landlords that do not actively use or occupy the assets acquired or improved with the loan proceeds (except when the property is leased to the business at zero profit for the property's owners)

Life insurance companies:

Businesses located in a foreign country (businesses in the U.S. owned by aliens may qualify)

Businesses engaged in pyramid sale distribution plans, where a participant's primary incentive is based on the sales made by an ever-increasing number of participants

Businesses deriving more than one-third of gross annual revenue from legal gambling activities

Businesses engaged in any illegal activity

Private clubs and businesses that limit the number of memberships for reasons other than capacity

Government-owned entities:

Businesses principally engaged in teaching, instructing, counseling or indoctrinating religion or religious beliefs, whether in a religious or secular setting

Consumer and marketing cooperatives (producer cooperatives are eligible)

Loan packagers earning more than one third of their gross annual revenue from packaging SBA loans

Businesses in which the lender or CDC, or any of its associates owns an equity interest

Businesses that present live performances of an indecent sexual nature or derive directly or indirectly more 2.5 percent of gross revenue through the sale of products or services, or the presentation of any depictions or displays, of an indecent sexual nature

Businesses primarily engaged in political or lobbying activities

Speculative businesses (such as oil exploration)

There are also eligibility factors for financial assistance based on the activities of the owners and the historical operation of the business. As such, the business cannot have been:

A business that caused the government to have incurred a loss related to a prior business debt

A business owned 20 percent or more by a person associated with a different business that caused the government to have incurred a loss related to a prior business debt

A business owned 20 percent or more by a person who is incarcerated, on probation, on parole, or has been indicted for a felony or a crime of moral depravity

Special Considerations:

Special considerations apply to some types of businesses and individuals, which include:

Franchises are eligible except when a franchiser retains power to control operations to such an extent as to equate to an employment contract; the franchisee must have the right to profit from efforts commensurate with ownership

Recreational facilities and clubs are eligible if the facilities are open to the general public, or in membership-only situations, membership is not selectively denied or restricted to any particular groups

Farms and agricultural businesses are eligible, but these applicants should first explore Farm Service Agency (FSA) programs, particularly if the applicant has a prior or existing relationship with FSA

Fishing vessels are eligible, but those seeking funds for the construction or reconditioning of vessels with a cargo capacity of five tons or more must first request financing from the National Marine Fisheries Service

Privately owned medical facilities including hospitals, clinics, emergency outpatient facilities, and medical and dental laboratories are eligible; recovery and nursing homes are also eligible, provided they are licensed by the appropriate government agency and they provide more than room and board

An Eligible Passive Company (EPC) must use loan proceeds to acquire or lease, and/or improve or renovate, real or personal property that it leases to one or more operating companies and must not make any profit from conducting its activities

Legal aliens are eligible; however, consideration is given to status (e.g., resident, lawful temporary resident) in determining the business' degree of risk

Probation or parole: Applications will not be accepted from firms in which a principal is currently incarcerated, on parole, on probation or is a defendant in a criminal proceeding

Use of 7(a) Loan Proceeds

If you are awarded a 7(a) loan, you can use the loan proceeds to help finance a large variety of business purposes. However, there are a few restrictions. For example, proceeds can't be used to buy an asset to hold for its potential increased value or to reimburse an owner for the money they previously put into their business.

Basic uses for 7(a) loan proceeds include:

- To provide long-term working capital to use to pay operational expenses, accounts payable and/or to purchase inventory
- Short-term working capital needs, including seasonal financing, contract performance, construction financing and exporting
- Revolving funds based on the value of existing inventory and receivables, under special conditions
- To purchase equipment, machinery, furniture, fixtures, supplies or materials
- To purchase real estate, including land and buildings
- To construct a new building or renovate an existing building
- To establish a new business or assist in the acquisition, operation or expansion of an existing business
- To refinance existing business debt, under certain conditions

SBA loans cannot be used for these purposes:

- To refinance existing debt where the lender is in a position to sustain a loss and SBA would take over that loss through refinancing

- To affect a partial change of business ownership or a change that will not benefit the business

- To permit the reimbursement of funds owed to any owner, including any equity injection or injection of capital to continue the business until the SBA-backed loan is disbursed

- To repay delinquent state or federal withholding taxes or other funds that should be held in trust or escrow

- For a purpose that is not considered to be a sound business purpose as determined by SBA

- If you are unsure whether or not your anticipated use of funds is allowed, check with your SBA-approved lender

7(a) Loan Processing Time

There are two 7(a) loan process options with different time frames. In addition to standard procedures, SBA Express processing offers an expedited turnaround.

About SBA Express

SBA Express gives small business borrowers an accelerated turnaround time for SBA review. A response to an application will be given within 36 hours. SBA Express generally follows SBA's standards for the 7(a)-loan program.

The maximum loan amount is $350,000.

The maximum SBA guaranty percentage is 50%.

Lenders and borrowers can negotiate the interest rate. Rates can be fixed or variable and are tied to the prime rate (as published in The Wall Street Journal), LIBOR, or the optional peg rate (published quarterly in the Federal Register) but they may not exceed SBA's maximum rates. Lenders may charge up to 6.5 % over the base rate for loans of $50,000 or less, and up to 4.5 % over the base rate for loans over $50,000.

Revolving lines of credit are available up to seven years.

Lenders primarily use their own forms and procedures for loan processing.

Lenders are not required to take collateral for loans up to $25,000; however, they may use their existing collateral policy for loans over $25,000 and up to $350,000.

Microloan Program

The Microloan program provides loans up to $50,000 to help small businesses and certain not-for-profit childcare centers start up and expand. The average microloan is about $13,000.

The U.S. Small Business Administration provides funds to specially designated intermediary lenders, which are nonprofit community-based organizations with experience in lending as well as management and technical assistance. These intermediaries administer the Microloan program for eligible borrowers.

Eligibility Requirements

Each intermediary lender has its own lending and credit requirements. Generally, intermediaries require some type of collateral as well as the personal guarantee of the business owner.

Use of Microloan Proceeds

Microloans can be used for:

- ❖ Working capital
- ❖ Inventory or supplies
- ❖ Furniture or fixtures
- ❖ Machinery or equipment

Proceeds from an SBA microloan cannot be used to pay existing debts or to purchase real estate.

Repayment Terms, Interest Rates, and Fees:

Loan repayment terms vary according to several factors:

- ❖ Loan amount
- ❖ Planned use of funds
- ❖ Requirements determined by the intermediary lender
- ❖ Needs of the small business borrower
- ❖ The maximum repayment term allowed for an SBA microloan is six years.

Interest rates vary, depending on the intermediary lender and costs to the intermediary from the U.S. Treasury. Generally, these rates will be between 8 and 13 percent.

Application Process

Microloans are available through certain nonprofit, community-based organizations that are experienced in lending and business management assistance. If you apply for SBA microloan financing, you may be required to fulfill training or planning requirements before your loan application is considered. This business training is designed to help you launch or expand your business.

Find a Microloan Provider:

To apply for a Microloan, you must work with an SBA approved intermediary in your area. Approved intermediaries make all credit decisions on SBA microloans. For more information, you can contact your local SBA District Office or view the list of Participating Microloan Intermediary Lenders.

CAP Lines

The CAP lines program for loans up to $5 million is designed to help small businesses meet their short-term and cyclical working capital needs. The programs can be used to finance seasonal working capital needs; finance the direct costs of performing certain construction, service and supply contracts, subcontracts, or purchase orders; finance the direct cost associated with commercial and residential construction; or provide general working capital lines of credit that have specific requirements for repayment.

There are four distinct loan programs under the CAP lines umbrella:

The Contract Loan Program finances the cost associated with contracts, subcontracts or purchase orders. Proceeds can be disbursed before the work begins. If used for one contract or subcontract when all the expenses are incurred before the buyer pays, it will generally not revolve. If used for more than one contract or subcontract, or for contracts and subcontracts where the buyer pays before all work is done, the line of credit can revolve. The loan maturity is usually based on the length of the contract, but no more than 10 years. Contract payments are generally sent directly to the lender, but alternative structures are available.

The Seasonal Line of Credit Program supports the buildup of inventory, accounts receivable or labor and materials above normal usage for seasonal inventory. The business must have been in business for a period of 12 months and must be able to demonstrate that it has a definite established seasonal pattern. The loan may be used over again after a "clean up" period of 30 days to finance activity for a new season. These loans also may have a maturity of up to five years. The business may not have another seasonal line of credit outstanding, but may have other lines for non-seasonal working capital needs.

The Builders Line Program provides financing for small contractors or developers to construct or rehabilitate residential or commercial property that will be sold to a third party that is not known at the time construction/rehabilitation begins. Loan maturity is generally three years, but can be extended up to five years, if necessary, to facilitate the sale of the property. Proceeds are used solely for direct expenses of acquisition, immediate construction and/or significant rehabilitation of the residential or commercial structures. Land purchase can be included if it does not exceed 20 percent of the loan proceeds. Up to five percent of the proceeds can be used for community improvements that benefit the overall property.

The Working Capital Line of Credit Program is a revolving line of credit (up to $5,000,000) that provides short-term working capital. Businesses that generally use these lines provide credit to their customers or have inventory as their major asset. Disbursements are generally based on the size of a borrower's accounts receivable and/or inventory. Repayment comes from the collection of accounts receivable or sale of inventory. The specific structure is negotiated with the lender. There may be extra servicing and monitoring of the collateral for which the lender can charge additional fees to the borrower.

About Venture Capital

Venture capital is a type of equity financing that addresses the funding needs of entrepreneurial companies that for reasons of size, assets, and stage of development cannot seek capital from more traditional sources, such as public markets and banks. Venture capital investments are generally made as cash in exchange for shares and an active role in the invested company.

Venture capital differs from traditional financing sources in that venture capital typically:

- ❖ Focuses on young, high-growth companies
- ❖ Invests equity capital, rather than debt
- ❖ Takes higher risks in exchange for potential higher returns
- ❖ Has a longer investment horizon than traditional financing?
- ❖ Actively monitors portfolio companies via board participation, strategic marketing, governance, and capital structure.

Successful long-term growth for most businesses is dependent upon the availability of equity capital. Lenders generally require some equity cushion or security (collateral) before they will lend to a small business. A lack of equity limits the debt financing available to businesses. Additionally, debt financing requires the ability to service the debt through current interest payments. These funds are then not available to grow the business.

Venture capital provides businesses a financial cushion. However, equity providers have the last call against the company's assets. In view of this lower priority and the usual lack of a current pay requirement, equity providers require a higher rate of return/return on investment (ROI) than lenders receive.

Grants

The federal government does NOT provide grants for starting and expanding a business.

Government grants are funded by your tax dollars and therefore require very stringent compliance and reporting measures to ensure the money is well spent. As you can imagine, grants are not given away indiscriminately.

Grants from the federal government are only available to non-commercial organizations, such as non-profits and educational institutions in areas such as, medicine, education, scientific research and technology development. The federal government also provides grants to state and local governments to assist them with economic development.

Some business grants are available through state and local programs, non-profit organizations and other groups. For example, some states provide grants for expanding child care centers; creating energy efficient technology; and developing marketing campaigns for tourism. These grants are not necessarily free money, and usually require the recipient to match funds or combine the grant with other forms of financing such as a loan. The amount of the grant money available varies with each business and each grantor.

If you are not one of these specialized businesses, both federal and state government agencies provide financial assistance programs, which help small business owners obtain low-interest loans and venture capital financing from commercial lenders.

Chapter Ten

Last Minute questions and jitters before taking the final step

Starting your own business can be an exciting and rewarding experience. It can offer numerous advantages such as being your own boss, setting your own schedule and making a living doing something you enjoy. But, becoming a successful entrepreneur requires thorough planning, creativity and hard work.

Consider whether you have the following characteristics and skills commonly associated with successful entrepreneurs:

Comfortable with taking risks: Being your own boss also means you're the one making tough decisions. Entrepreneurship involves uncertainty. Do you avoid uncertainty in life at all costs? If yes, then entrepreneurship may not be the best fit for you. Do you enjoy the thrill of taking calculated risks? Then read on.

Independent: Entrepreneurs have to make a lot of decisions on their own. If you find you can trust your instincts and you're not afraid of rejection every now and then you could be on your way to being an entrepreneur.

Persuasive: You may have the greatest idea in the world, but if you cannot persuade customers, employees and potential lenders or partners, you may find entrepreneurship to be challenging. If you enjoy public speaking, engage new people with ease and find you make compelling arguments grounded in facts, it's likely you're poised to make your idea succeed.

Able to negotiate: As a small business owner, you will need to negotiate everything from leases to contract terms to rates. Polished negotiation skills will help you save money and keep your business running smoothly.

Creative: Are you able to think of new ideas? Can you imagine new ways to solve problems? Entrepreneurs must be able to think creatively. If you have insights on how to take advantage of new opportunities, entrepreneurship may be a good fit.

Supported by others: Before you start a business, it's important to have a strong support system in place. You'll be forced to make many important decisions, especially in the first months of opening your business. If you do not have a support network of people to help you, consider finding a business mentor. A business mentor is someone who is experienced, successful and willing to provide advice and guidance. Read the Steps to Finding a Mentor article for help on finding and working with a mentor.

Still think you have what it takes to be an entrepreneur and start a new business? Great! Now ask yourself these 20 questions to help ensure you've thought about the right financial and business details. These questions are located on the Small Business Administration website as well; I also would like to point out that I too answered these questions before moving forward with a business plan to start my own business.

- Why am I starting a business?
- What kind of business do I want?
- Who is my ideal customer?
- What products or services will my business provide?
- Am I prepared to spend the time and money needed to get my business started?
- What differentiates my business idea and the products or services I will provide from others in the market?
- Where will my business be located?
- How many employees will I need?
- What types of suppliers do I need?
- How much money do I need to get started?
- Will I need to get a loan?
- How soon will it take before my products or services are available?
- How long do I have until I start making a profit?
- Who is my competition?
- How will I price my product compared to my competition?
- How will I set up the legal structure of my business?
- What taxes do I need to pay?

Basics of Business

> ➢ What kind of insurance do I need?
>
> ➢ How will I manage my business?
>
> ➢ How will I advertise my business?

Understand Your Market

To run a successful business, you need to learn about your customers, your competitors and your industry. Market research is the process of analyzing data to help you understand which products and services are in demand, and how to be competitive. Market research can also provide valuable insight to help you:

- Reduce business risks
- Spot current and upcoming problems in your industry
- Identify sales opportunities
- How to Conduct Market Research

Before you start your business, understand the basics of market research by following these steps:

- Identify Official Government Sources of Market and Industry Data

- ❖ The government offers a wealth of data and information about businesses, industries and economic conditions that can aid in conducting market research.

- ❖ **These sources provide valuable information about your customers and competitors:**
  - ❖ Economic Indicators
  - ❖ Employment Statistics
  - ❖ Income and Earnings
  - ❖ Identify Additional Sources of Analysis
- ❖ Trade groups, business magazines, academic institutions and other third parties gather and analyze research data about business trends. Use Internet and database searches to find information related to your location and industry.

Understand the International Marketplace

Today's economy is a globalized marketplace, so it's important to understand the international factors that influence your business. These resources will help you to research potential international markets for your products or services:

- ❖ Market Research Guide for Exporters
- ❖ Identifies resources for business owners seeking to sell their products abroad.
- ❖ Country Market Research
- ❖ Reports on trade issues in countries across the globe.
- ❖ BuyUSA.gov
- ❖ Helps U.S. companies find new international business partners.

Glossary

- **Accounting**- profession of maintaining the financial records of a business, including bookkeeping.

- **Articles of incorporation**- What are 'Articles of Incorporation' A set of formal documents filed with a government body to legally document the creation of a corporation.

- **Bounced check-** transitive and intransitive verb to refuse payment of a check, or be refused by a bank, because there is insufficient money in the account on which it is drawn

- **Business plan-** A business plan is an essential roadmap for business success. This living document generally projects 3-5 years ahead and outlines the route a company intends to take

- **Business law**- Business law is a broad area of law. It covers many different types of laws and many different topics.

- **C-corporation** - A corporation (sometimes referred to as a C corporation) is an independent legal entity owned by shareholders.

- **Cash processing**- money in the form of coins or bills as distinct from money orders or credit

- **Checks**- a small printed form that, when filled out and signed, instructs a bank to pay a specific sum of money to the person named on it.

- **Copyright**- Copyright is a form of protection provided by the laws of the United States to the creators of original works including literary works, movies, musical works.

- **Credit card**- a card issued by a bank or business that allows somebody to purchase goods and services and pay for them later, often with interest

Glossary

- **E-Commerce**- E-commerce is a transaction of buying or selling online. Electronic commerce draws on technologies such as mobile commerce, electronic funds transfer.

- **Entrepreneur**- Entrepreneur definition, a person who organizes and manages any enterprise, especially a business, usually with considerable initiative and risk.

- **Ethical**- consistent with agreed principles of correct moral conduct

- **Ethics**- a system of moral principles governing the appropriate conduct for a person or group.

- **FTC**- The Federal Trade Commission (FTC) is an independent agency of the United States government, established in 1914 by the Federal Trade Commission Act.

- **Fiduciary**- relating to or depending on confidence in a government for the value of fiat money.

- **Financial**- relating to or involving money or finance

- **Franchise**- an agreement or license to sell a company's products exclusively in a particular area or to operate a business that carries that company's name.

- **Grants**- a sum of money given by the government or some other organization to fund such things as education or research.

- **Hosting**- Hosting provides companies with transparent, always-on compliant managed cloud solutions backed by the industries best team.

- **IRS**- The Internal Revenue Service (IRS) is the revenue service of the United States federal government. The government agency is a bureau of the Department of the Treasury

Glossary

- **Income**- the amount of money received over a period of time either as payment for work, goods, or services, or as profit on capital.

- **Incorporated**- formed into a legal corporation in the U.S.

- **Incorporation**- Incorporation is the legal process used to form a corporate entity or company. A corporation is a separate legal entity.

- **Insufficient funds**- Occurs when an account cannot provide adequate funds to satisfy the demand of a payment. Also, referred to as "non-sufficient funds", or "NSF". Insufficient funds

- **Insurance**- an arrangement by which a company gives customers financial protection against loss or harm such as theft or illness in return for payment premium

- **LLC**- A limited liability company (LLC) is the United States-specific form of a private limited company. It is a business structure that combines the pass-through taxation

- **Liability**-: the state of being legally responsible for something: the state of being liable for something.

- **Loan**- an amount of money given to somebody on the condition that it will be paid back later.

Basics of Business

- **Market analysis-** Market segmentation. Market segmentation is the basis for a differentiated market analysis.

- **Marketing-** Marketing is a form of communication between you and your customers with the goal of selling your product or service to them.

Glossary

- **Market share-** The percentage of an industry or market's total sales that is earned by a particular company over a specified time period.

- **Metaphor-** A metaphor is a figure of speech that refers, for rhetorical effect, to one thing by mentioning another thing. It may provide clarity or identify hidden similarities

- **Multifaceted-** having many different parts: having many facets

- **Multitude-** 1. A very great number. 2. The masses; the populace: the concerns of the multitude.

- **NSF-** Non-Sufficient Funds

- **Nexus-** a connection or link associating two or more people or things.

- ➢ **Partnership-** A partnership is an arrangement where parties, known as partners, agree to cooperate to advance their mutual interests.

- ➢ **Platform-** Computing platform means in general sense, where any piece of software is executed. It may be the hardware or the operating system.

- ➢ **SBA-** Small Business Administration

- ➢ **S-Corporation-** An S Corporation (also referred to as an S corp) is a special type of corporation created through an IRS tax election.

- ➢ **Sectary of state-** Each division of the Secretary of State's Office provides diverse services and information

Glossary

- **Small Business Administration-** We support America's small businesses. The SBA connects entrepreneurs with lenders and funding to help them plan, start and grow their business.

- **Social-** relating to human society and its modes of organization: social classes; social problems; a social issue.

- **Society-** a structured community of people bound together by similar traditions, institutions, or nationality

- **Social responsibility-** Corporate social responsibility is imperative, as most consumers and job seekers consider how businesses deal with their environmental, social and economic impacts.

- **Survey**- take a general or comprehensive view of or appraise, as a situation, area of study, etc.

- **Taxation**- The rate of her taxation increased as her promotion provided her with a huge boost in income, thereby causing her to owe more to the government

- **Website**- A website is a collection of related web pages, including multimedia content, typically identified with a common domain name, and published on at least one web server.

Bibliography

Taxes, Category: Managing Your. "Compare Tax Considerations by Business Type." BizFilings. Accessed April 04, 2017. http://www.bizfilings.com/learn/taxes-business-types.aspx.

Taxes, Category: Managing Your. "Understanding State Corporate Taxes." BizFilings. Accessed April 04, 2017. http://www.bizfilings.com/learn/state-corporate-taxes.aspx.

"Buying Insurance | The U.S. Small Business Administration." Small Business Administration. Accessed April 04, 2017. https://www.sba.gov/managing-business/running-business/insurance/buying-insurance.

"Extending Credit to Your Customers | The U.S. Small Business Administration." Small Business Administration. Accessed April 04, 2017. https://www.sba.gov/managing-business/running-business/managing-business-finances-accounting/extending-credit-your-customers.

Brown, Betty Jean., and John E. Clow. Glencoe introduction to business. New York, NY: Glencoe/McGraw-Hill, 2008.

Strydom, J. W. Introduction to marketing. Cape Town, South Africa: Juta, 2014.

Dyer, L. M., and C. A. Ross. "Advising the Small Business Client." International Small Business Journal 25, no. 2 (2007): 130-51. doi:10.1177/0266242607074517.

Bibliography

"Common sense business ethics." For Business Ethics: 10-9. doi:10.4324/9780203458457_chapter_2.

Pierre, Samuel. "Mobile Electronic Commerce." Encyclopedia of E-Commerce, E-Government, and Mobile Commerce: 786-91. doi:10.4018/978-1-59140-799-7.ch126.

"America's next jobless." The Economist (US), February 6, 1988.

"Stamps.com Garners Recognition on Forbes Magazine's List of America's Best Small Companies." Entertainment Close-up, October 22, 2013.

"Malcolm Forbes: The Man Who Had Everything." The Economist (US), January 19, 1991.

Ward, Dan. "Doing less with more: the pitfalls of overfunding." Defense AT & L, November 1, 2004.

"Value of small business loans outstanding in the United States: United States." 2016. doi:10.1787/fin_sme_ent-2016-table305-en.

www.ingramcontent.com/pod-product-compliance
Lightning Source LLC
Chambersburg PA
CBHW080940170526
45158CB00008B/2321